PATRICIA LAUBER

ALLIGATORS

A Success Story

▼ ▲ ▼ ▲ ▼

illustrated by Lou Silva

A Redfeather Book

Henry Holt and Company ▲ *New York*

Henry Holt and Company, Inc. / *Publishers since 1866*
115 West 18th Street / New York, New York 10011

Henry Holt is a registered trademark of Henry Holt and Company, Inc.

Published in Canada by Fitzhenry & Whiteside Ltd.,
195 Allstate Parkway, Markham, Ontario L3R 4T8.

Library of Congress Cataloging-in-Publication Data
Lauber, Patricia.
Alligators: a success story / Patricia Lauber; illustrated by Lou Silva.
(A Redfeather Book)—Includes index.
Summary: Examines the life cycle of the alligator from egg to adult
and analyzes its significance in the ecological balance of nature.
1. American alligator—Juvenile literature. [1. Alligators.]
I. Silva, Lou, ill. II. Title. III. Series: Redfeather books.
QL666.C925L37 1993 597.98—dc20 93-3302

ISBN 0-8050-1909-X (hardcover)
10 9 8 7 6 5 4 3 2 1
ISBN 0-8050-4258-X (paperback)
10 9 8 7 6 5 4 3 2 1

First published in hardcover in 1993
by Henry Holt and Company, Inc.
First Redfeather paperback edition, 1995

Printed in the United States of America on acid-free paper.∞

The author wishes to thank Kent A. Vliet, Ph.D., of the
Department of Zoology, University of Florida, for his careful
reading of the manuscript and helpful suggestions.

This book is based in part on an earlier one by Patricia Lauber,
Who Needs Alligators? [Garrard Publishing Company, 1974].

Permission for use of the following photographs is gratefully acknowledged:
Patricia Caulfield, pp. 4, 12, 44, 56; Jack Couffer/Bruce Coleman, p. 36;
Kerry T. Givens/Tom Stack and Associates, p. 20;
Wendell Metzen/Bruce Coleman, p. 28.

ALLIGATORS
A Success Story

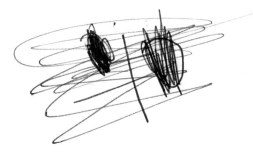

Contents

ALLIGATORS
A Success Story

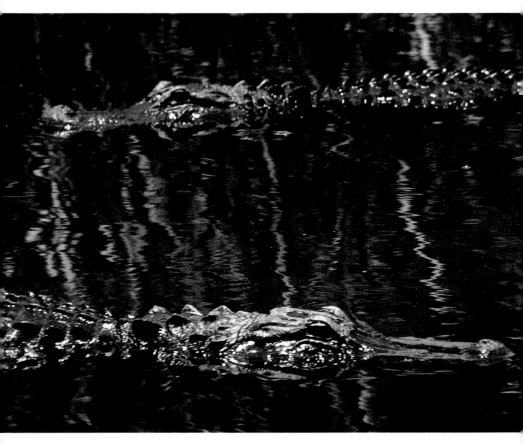

Afloat in the water, an alligator could easily be mistaken for a log.

▾1▾

Dinosaurs, Dragons, and Alligators

At first glance the pond seems empty of life. You see nothing except a big log that floats, half sunken, in the water. Most of it is just a long dark shape beneath the surface.

Suddenly the dark shape comes to life and paddles slowly toward the bank of the pond. It is an alligator, not a log. The alligator climbs out of the water and stands for a few minutes, swinging its big head and looking around. When it yawns, it shows a mouthful of sharp white teeth. It lies down and stretches out in the sun. Its stubby legs

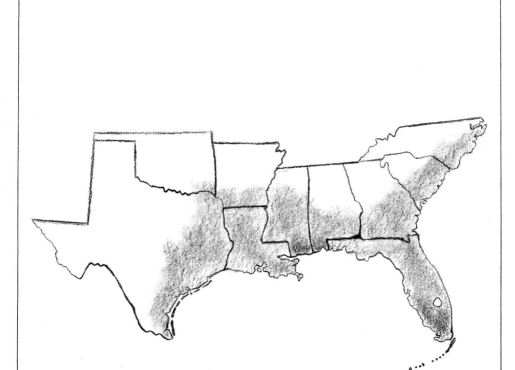

The Range of
the American Alligator

Alligators live where winters are mild. They cannot survive freezing temperatures. The shaded area of the map shows the range of the American alligator. The largest numbers live in Florida and Louisiana.

and thick toes hug the ground. Its eyes close. Because its jaws curve up, it seems to smile.

Alligators often sun themselves to warm up, just as snakes, lizards, and turtles do. All these animals are reptiles. And a reptile's body cannot make its own heat or keep a steady temperature the way our bodies do. A reptile takes its heat from an outside source—from the sun's rays or from sun-warmed earth, rock, or water. When a reptile starts to feel too hot, it moves to a cooler place. The alligator will slide back into its pond when it has had enough sun.

Half close your eyes and it is easy to imagine that you are looking at a dragon. In a way, you are. The dragons of fairy tales and myths may well have been alligators and crocodiles that men had met and fought. Sometimes the breath of a bellowing alligator can be seen. The cloudy breath looks like smoke. Smoke suggests fire— and so, as stories were told over and over, dragons became creatures that breathed fire.

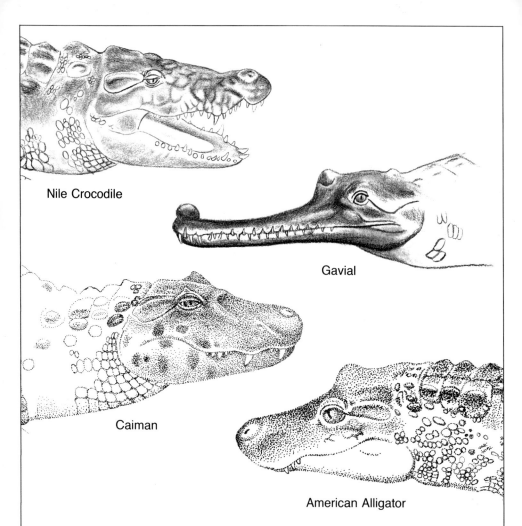

Nile Crocodile

Gavial

Caiman

American Alligator

The Alligator and Its Relatives

Alligators belong to a group of reptiles that are known as crocodilians. Scientists group the crocodilians in three families: crocodiles, alligators and caimans, and gavials. The best way to tell them apart is by the shape of the snout. There are more than 20 kinds of crocodilians in the world.

It's even easier to imagine that you are looking at a dinosaur. You aren't, of course, but you are looking at a relative of the dinosaurs. Alligators and dinosaurs share the same family tree. About 250 million years ago, animals called thecodonts roamed the earth. Over time some developed into other kinds of animals. Among them were alligators and crocodiles—and dinosaurs.

For millions and millions of years, alligators and crocodiles lived in a world ruled by dinosaurs. They competed with dinosaurs for food and living space. Then, about 65 million years ago, something happened and the dinosaurs died out. Alligators and crocodiles did not—they survived. They lived on, surviving many other great changes on earth. Natural scientists call them successful animals.

The alligator you are watching looks like the crocodilians that lived with dinosaurs. And that is one of the great pleasures of watching alligators. It's like visiting the world of dinosaurs.

An Ancient Relative

Crocodilians shared the world of dinosaurs. Some crocodilians were small—only 12 to 20 inches long. Some were middle sized—3 to 10 feet long. And some were huge. *Deinosuchus* was one of those, growing perhaps 50 feet in length. *Deinosuchus* lived about 75 million years ago. Mostly it ate fish and turtles that made the mistake of coming close to its huge jaws. But this crocodilian could also bring down, kill, and eat a large dinosaur.

▾2▾

At Home in the Water

All alligators leave the water from time to time, as they do when sunning themselves. But an alligator's body is designed for water, where the alligator spends most of its life.

Eyes, ears, and nose are set in the top of the alligator's head. They are above water when the alligator swims at the surface or floats. It can see, hear, and smell. All its senses are good—and that

An alligator floats half-sunken in the water but can see, hear, and smell because its eyes, ears, and nostrils are set in the top of its head.

is another thing that makes the alligator success-ful.

When an alligator dives, several things happen. The throat closes, so the alligator can open its jaws to snatch prey without taking water into its lungs. Flaps of skin close the ear openings and keep water out. Muscles close the nostrils. A thin, soft covering slips across the eyes. The covering is a third eyelid. It protects the eyes from water.

An alligator's feet are partly webbed. They serve as paddles when the alligator swims slowly and cruises through the water.

To swim fast, an alligator uses its long, powerful tail. It tucks its legs against its body and sweeps its tail back and forth. The tail moves with a wavy motion, like a snake. An alligator can swim faster than a person can paddle a canoe. It can swerve from side to side or shoot ahead to catch a fish.

On land, alligators are somewhat clumsy.

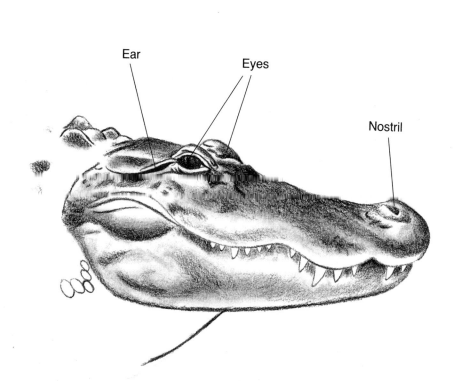

Ear

Eyes

Nostril

An Alligator's Senses

An alligator's eyes, ears, and nostrils are set in the top of its head. The alligator can see, hear, and smell when it is swimming at the surface or floating. All its senses are good. Alligators can see well at night, for the same reason that cats can. At the back of each eyeball is a thin layer of cells that acts like a mirror, gathering and reflecting dim light. Shine a flashlight on an alligator at night and you will see what looks like a pair of glowing coals—the alligator's eyes.

Their bodies are long and heavy, and their legs are short. Usually an alligator waddles along with its tail dragging on the ground. If startled, an alligator can move fast for a short distance. It pulls itself up so that its body clears the ground. Only the tip of its tail drags. The alligator scuttles away on its short legs. If possible, it heads for water and slides in.

How an Alligator Moves

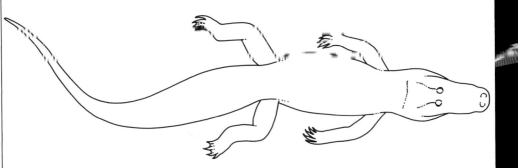

To swim slowly, an alligator paddles with its partly webbed feet.

To swim fast, it tucks its legs against its body, becoming streamlined, and sweeps its powerful tail back and forth.

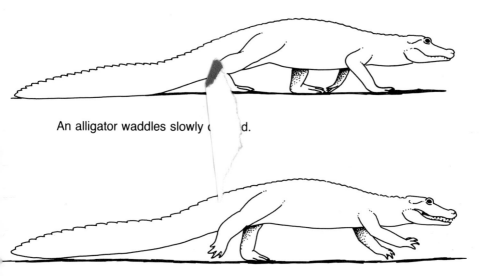

An alligator waddles slowly d.

If startled, the alligator pulls its body up and dashes along, about as fast as a man can run.

Many alligators have no need to travel much by land. The places where they live have water all year round. But some swamps and marshes go dry in spring, which is mating time for alligators. There females may leave their ponds and travel half a mile by land, bellowing for mates. Males roam widely, traveling several miles between ponds. Like the alligators in wet places, each bellows with a roar like thunder. Each is announcing himself as he searches for a mate. Each is claiming the territory around him.

Sometimes two males meet, both claiming the same territory. They glare at each other, whacking their tails from side to side and hissing angrily. Then they rush at each other. One may drive the other away, or they may fight. Locked together, they wrestle. They roll over and over. Each tries to close his jaws on the other. A male may lose a leg or part of his tail in the fight. Even so, he can still manage to live. Alligators are tough—and that is another thing that makes them successful.

When the battle ends, the winner moves on, bellowing and announcing himself, listening for a female to answer with a bellow of her own.

Alligators almost always court and mate in water. In courting, the female rubs the male's head, nuzzles his neck, and pushes him gently. She slides over his back. Each strokes the other's head. They bump noses softly. After mating, the male may spend a day or two with the female before moving on. Or he may stay with her during nest building, egg laying, and hatching. Nest building begins about a month after mating.

Having broken out of its shell, this young alligator is taking its first look at the world.

▾3▾

The Nest and Eggs

An alligator nest is a large mound of grass, leaves, twigs, reeds, and other plant material. A female may build a nest near the water where she lives or she may repair her old nest.

A female spends several hours a day working on her nest. She collects material for it by biting off some plants and tearing others out by their roots. Using her legs or her snout, she pushes the plant material onto the nest. She packs it in place by crawling over it, using the weight of her body to press the material into the mound. She makes

The Nest

Height: 2 to 3 feet

Diameter: about 6 feet

Eggs: usually 25 to 35, 2 to 3 inches long

Nest material: grass and other plants, twigs, mud

A female alligator may build a new nest or she may repair her old nest. The nest is always near water. Most females guard their nests against animals that would eat the eggs.

trip after trip to the mound and often walks around it, inspecting her work. When she has finished, the mound is a sturdy, cone-shaped nest that stands two or three feet high and measures about six feet across.

The female climbs to the top, where she scoops out a big hollow with her hind feet. She spreads her legs and begins to lay her eggs. An alligator usually lays 25 to 35 eggs that are 2 to 3 inches long. Their shells are hard and white.

When she has laid all her eggs, the alligator covers them with more plant material. She smooths the nest with her body by crawling around and around it.

For the next two months the alligator stays close to her nest. She guards it against raccoons, bears, and other animals that like to eat alligator eggs.

The weeks pass. The summer sun warms the air and nest. The nest itself also warms the eggs, because plant material gives off heat as it rots.

Inside each shell, a tiny alligator is taking shape and growing.

The sex of the young depends on how warm the eggs are during their first few weeks. If the female builds her nest in the shade, the average temperature is likely to be 86 degrees Fahrenheit or lower. The young in these eggs will be females. If she builds her nest in the sun, the average is likely to be 93 degrees or higher. The young in these eggs will be males. Usually most of the young from one nest are of the same sex.

Does a female make a choice? Does she decide whether to build her nest in a sunny place or a shady one? Or is the nest site a matter of chance? No one knows, but scientists who study alligators are hoping to find out.

Hatching begins in late summer, about two months after the eggs were laid. By then some young have grown too big for their shells. The shells swell, then crack. But the young alligators are still not out. Inside the shell is a thin, tough

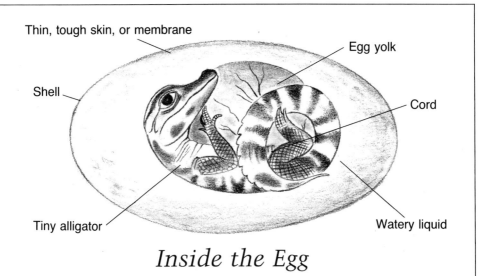

Thin, tough skin, or membrane

Egg yolk

Shell

Cord

Tiny alligator

Watery liquid

Inside the Egg

A tiny alligator develops with its back curled against the shell and its tail tucked between its legs. It is cushioned and kept from drying out by watery liquid inside the membrane. It receives nourishment from the egg yolk, to which it is linked by a cord. Air passes through the shell, which has pores. Oxygen is taken up by blood vessels in the membrane and then by blood vessels in the tiny alligator.

skin. Each tiny alligator has a sharp tooth, which it uses to slit this skin. Then it presses against the shell with its head. The shell breaks open. As they hatch, the young grunt.

The mother alligator is nearby. Hearing the calls of her young, she climbs to the top of the nest and opens it with her jaws. The young alligators wiggle out of their eggshells. Sometimes the mother helps the young to hatch. She takes an egg in her mouth and cracks the shell by pressing it between her tongue and the roof of her mouth. Alligators have huge, powerful jaws. But the mother helps the young so gently that they are not injured.

A newly hatched alligator is eight inches long and weighs less than two ounces. It has a black body, with white stripes that later turn yellow.

Within three or four days all the eggs hatch. Some of the tiny alligators make their own way out of the nest to water. Some may be led by their mother, or she may carry them in her open jaws. Once they are in the water, they start to swim around their mother. They follow her. They crawl onto her head and back to rest or sun themselves. She keeps watch for animals that might eat them. And that is another thing that makes alligators successful—they are good mothers who take care of their eggs and young.

▾4▾

Eating and Being Eaten

lligators are hunters, and newly hatched young soon learn to catch their own food. They hunt and eat minnows, tadpoles, small crabs, and water beetles. They gulp down flies and moths that have fallen into the water. But they themselves are also hunted and eaten by many animals.

Raccoons, bobcats, mink, and otters are always ready to make a meal of a young alligator. So are snapping turtles, bullfrogs, garfish, black bass, and the snakes called cottonmouths. The great

horned owl is quick to pounce on a young alligator. A wading bird will spear and swallow one.

When threatened, the young give a cry that
sounds like "Yurk!" If big alligators are nearby,
they rush to defend the young. Even so, many
young are eaten.

For their first two or three years, the young
stay near the places where they hatched out.
Then older alligators drive them away, and they
wander through swamps and marshes and along
roads and ditches. By now they are about three
feet long and have little to fear from other animals. Alligators do not start to mate until they
are six feet long—and perhaps nine or ten years
old.

As an alligator grows, new teeth keep pushing
out old ones. The teeth are hollow, and they are
not rooted in the jaw as ours are. An alligator
sheds and grows teeth all through its life. If it
lives to be fifty years old, it may have had as
many as six thousand teeth.

Jaws and Teeth

An alligator's powerful jaws are lined with 70 to 80 cone-shaped teeth. An alligator swallows small prey whole and tears off chunks of larger prey. It never chews its food.

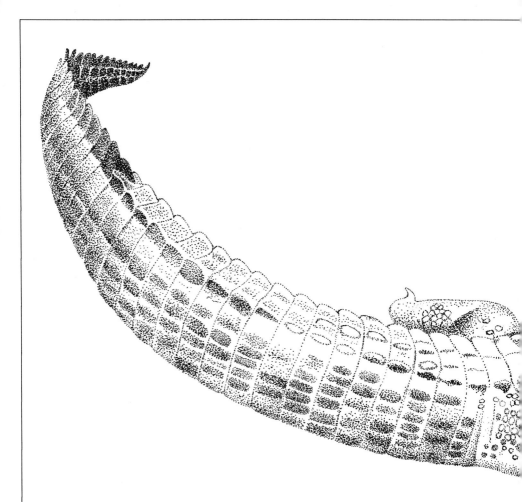

As well as using its jaws and teeth, an alligator uses its tail as a weapon. By swinging its strong, heavy tail it can bring down a large animal. Its back is armored with big bony plates, most of which have jagged ridges. Its legs, sides, and belly are covered with smooth horny scales. A big alligator can be harmed only by another big alligator or an armed human.

Weapons and Armor

Sharp teeth and powerful jaws are the tools that alligators use to catch their food. They swallow their food whole or in chunks, without chewing it. A big alligator can eat almost anything that flies, walks, swims, or crawls within reach of its jaws—fish, turtles, water birds, dogs, snakes, possums, raccoons, muskrats. And that is still another thing that makes alligators successful. Some animals can eat only a few kinds of food. If something happens to their food supply, they starve. An animal that is able to eat many kinds of food can survive both changes and hard times.

The teeth and jaws are fearsome, but alligators are not big eaters. Unlike animals that make their own heat, they don't need much food. Animals that make their own heat burn up food just keeping their bodies warm. Alligators do not make their own heat, and so they do not need to eat as much or as often as animals that do. In the cooler months, alligators may not eat at all.

Three or four good meals may be all they need in a whole year.

Because alligators do not eat all the time, many animals live near them without being harmed. And sometimes an alligator pond is the only place where they can live or find water to drink.

Alligators attack only when they feel threatened and eat only when they are hungry. This freshwater turtle, called a Peninsula cooter, can safely share the sun and log with an alligator that feels no need to eat.

▾5▾
Ponds of Life

Most rivers and lakes of the Southeast have water all year round. Swamps and marshes are different. They may be wet during the rainy season and fairly dry the rest of the year. In years when the rains do not come, they can go so dry that the ground cracks open. But even then, swamps and marshes are likely to be dotted with small ponds. The ponds are places where alligators live. They are deep enough to hold water when swamps and marshes dry up, because alligators keep digging them out.

Alligator Sounds

Alligators hiss as a warning when they are angry or feel threatened. In the mating season, males roar and bellow, calling for mates, and females answer with calls of their own. But males also bellow like thunder at other times. A loud noise—such as the boom of a plane going through the sound barrier—may set them off. Scientists are not sure what this bellowing means.

Water dance

Male alligators also do something called the water dance. A big male lifts his tail and head out of the water. He puffs up his throat, waves his tail, and drops down. Water dances around his body and he bellows.

Sometimes a male tilts his head above the water, then uses it to slap and splash the water noisily. The head slap may be done before, during, or after water dancing.

So far, scientists do not really know why alligators head slap and water dance.

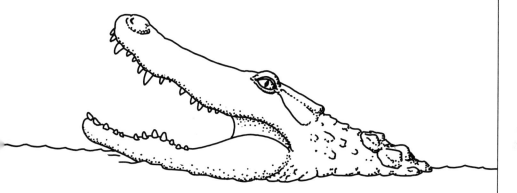

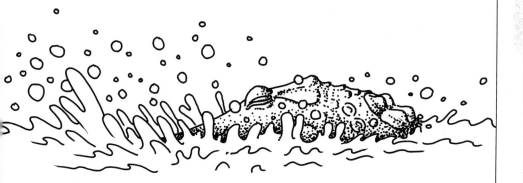

Head slap

By the time it is five or six feet long, an alligator is ready for a place of its own. In a marsh it may take over a pond that no longer has an owner. It may take a pond away from a smaller alligator. But sometimes an alligator makes its own pond.

It chooses a place where there is a hollow in the marsh, a place where ground water has collected. First it makes the hollow wider, tearing out grasses and reeds with its jaws, digging with its hind feet. It carries loose material away in its jaws. Then it makes the hollow deeper, digging out the bottom with its feet. Mud from the bottom mixes with the water in the hollow. The alligator uses its tail to sweep the muddy water out into the marsh. The finished pond may be as much as 30 feet across and be about 3 or 4 feet deep. It fills with ground water.

Some alligators also make dens. A den is a shelter and a safe place to be. The alligator usually spends the winter quietly in its den.

Sometimes a pond already has a den—a natural tunnel or cave or one built by another alligator. If not, the alligator digs a tunnel in the bank of the pond. It starts two or three feet below the surface of the water, tearing away plant roots and digging out dirt with its feet.

As the tunnel grows, the alligator digs with its teeth and pushes the loose material out of the tunnel with its hind feet. It also uses its tail to get rid of dirt. While backing out of the tunnel, it slowly sweeps its tail back and forth. The movement sets up a current that carries away the dirt.

Finally the alligator has a tunnel that may be as long as 20 feet. At the far end there is a space big enough for the alligator to turn around in. It also holds a pocket of air that seeps in through holes made by the roots of plants.

As long as the alligator lives there, it works on the pond. Without the alligator, the pond would fill in. With the alligator, the pond remains open.

Tunnel and Den

An alligator den has a turn-around space, with a pocket of air that seeps in through holes made by the roots of trees or other plants. An alligator retreats to its den if it feels threatened. It also spends the cool months of winter dozing in its den. It has little need to eat and may not come out until spring.

It holds water in the months when there is little rain, when the marsh begins to dry up. Then frogs, fish, and other water dwellers move toward the deeper parts of the marsh. Some move into alligator ponds. Other animals come to drink.

In the dry season alligator ponds are sources of life-giving water. And they are even more important in years when the rains fail to come, in years of drought. Then wet land becomes dry land, plants turn brown, shallow pools change to mud holes. An alligator pond may be the only water for miles around.

The ponds are packed with life. There are crabs, shrimp, snails. There are frogs, turtles, and water snakes. There are little fish and big fish. All need water to live in. They find it in the alligator pond. They also find food.

Tiny green plants grow in the water of the pond. Some of the animals feed on the plants. Other animals feed on the animals that eat the plants.

The Pond

Dirt dug from the pond and den forms a bank around the pond. Seeds lodge in the bank and grow into trees. The trees are a roosting and nesting place for birds. Flowers, fruits, and seeds provide food for birds and insects. Raccoons climb the trees to eat fruits and steal eggs from nests. In dry seasons or years of drought, the pond may be the only water for miles around. Many kinds of animals depend on it for life.

The pond has many visitors. Long-legged birds come to fish in its water. So do otters. Rabbits come to drink. Raccoons, opossums, and bob-cats come to feed and drink.

Then, of course, there is the alligator, which eats some of the animals that share its pond. Yet the pond is not a pond of death. It is a pond of life. Because it is there, many animals live through the drought. They are still alive when the rains come again.

And finally the rains do come. The dry land soaks up moisture. Hollows fill and become pools. Alligator ponds fill to the brim and over-flow. Shrimp, crabs, and fish spill out of the pond and spread through the marsh. Slowly the marsh comes back to life.

Could other animals survive without alliga-tors—without the ponds that alligators dig, with-out the ponds that alligators alone keep open? Perhaps some could, but many could not. Without alligators, the life of the marsh would be greatly changed.

And that was one reason why, some years ago, many people began to worry. They feared that alligators were in danger of being wiped out.

Living with Alligators

Once there were millions of alligators in the Southeast. But as the years passed, the number became smaller and smaller. There were two reasons for this.

One was the number of alligators that had been killed. Starting in the early 1800s, hunters began going into the swamps and marshes. They killed alligators for their hides, which were used to

When alligators travel in search of homes or mates, they may find themselves in places claimed by people, such as roads, swimming pools, or golf courses.

make handsome leather goods—shoes, luggage, wallets, and handbags. During the next 150 years, millions of alligators were killed. In some areas they were wiped out.

The other reason was that the number of people in the Southeast kept growing. Swamps and marshes were cleared and drained to make room for farms and homes. Alligators had fewer places to live.

Finally, in the 1960s, several states passed laws to protect alligators. The first were passed in Florida and Louisiana, which had always had the most alligators and the most hunters. A few years later the United States also took steps to protect alligators. Hunting was cut back or forbidden. In some places no one was allowed to sell goods made of alligator hide.

Alligators bounced back. Their numbers grew. They appeared in places where they hadn't been seen in years.

Clearly the laws had helped. But scientists also

noticed something interesting. Alligators grow slowly. Yet many of the ones they were counting were big. How could baby alligators have grown to this size in a few years? The answer, scientists decided, was that they hadn't. Threatened by hunters, the alligators must have gone into hiding. Once more they had proved to be successful survivors.

Today Louisiana has some 750,000 alligators, and Florida more than a million. Some hunting is allowed, but hunters may take no more than 25,000 alligators a year.

Most hunters sell the hides for leather, although some alligator meat is also sold. Still more hides come from alligator farms. The farmers use eggs harvested in the wild and kept warm until they hatch. The young are raised in pools. They are fed and cared for until they are four to six feet long. Then their hides are sent to market. With hides coming from farms, there is less reason for hunters to kill alligators in the wild.

With more alligators around, some do appear in places where they are not welcome. They are sometimes found on roads, in swimming pools and backyards, on golf courses and parking lots. These are considered a nuisance. Some are killed but others are taken away and turned loose in the wild.

And so, because alligators were protected, we can still look at them and dream of dragons and dinosaurs. We can also look at them and enjoy them as alligators, as animals that are a big success.

Index

Page numbers in *italic* refer to illustrations.